Did Yo

EXETER

A MISCELLANY

Compiled by Julia Skinner

With particular reference to the work of Dennis Needham

THE FRANCIS FRITH COLLECTION

www.francisfrith.com

Based on a book first published in the United Kingdom in 2005 by The Francis Frith Collection®

This edition published exclusively for Oakridge in 2009 ISBN 978-1-84589-444-3

British Library Cataloguing in Publication Data

Did You Know? Exeter - A Miscellany
Compiled by Julia Skinner
With particular reference to the work of Dennis Needham

The Francis Frith Collection
Frith's Barn, Teffont,
Salisbury, Wiltshire SP3 5QP
Tel: +44 (0) 1722 716 376
Email: info@francisfrith.co.uk
www.francisfrith.com

Printed and bound in Singapore

Front Cover: **EXETER, IN THE PORT 1896** 38036p

The colour-tinting is for illustrative purposes only, and is not intended to be historically accurate

AS WITH ANY HISTORICAL DATABASE, THE FRANCIS FRITH ARCHIVE IS CONSTANTLY BEING CORRECTED AND IMPROVED, AND THE PUBLISHERS WOULD WELCOME INFORMATION ON OMISSIONS OR INACCURACIES

CONTENTS

INTRODUCTION

The bustling modern city of Exeter stands on historic foundations. The area by the River Exe was settled by Celtic people called the Dumnonii. Around AD 55 the Romans established a town here as a base for the Second Augustan Legion, naming it Isca Dumnoniorum. Remains of the Roman walls can still be seen around the city, with a particularly good example at Southernhay, and archaeological excavations have discovered the site of one of the largest bath houses ever found in Roman Britain in the cathedral yard. Exeter suffered several attacks by the Vikings (or Danes) and was the last town in England to hold out against William the Conqueror, who besieged the town for eighteen days in 1068 before the townspeople were forced to surrender. The pride of Exeter is its magnificent cathedral, famed for its stone sculpture and woodcarvings, the Bishop's Throne, the astronomical clock, the twin Norman towers, the wonderful vaulted roof (the longest stretch of Gothic vaulting in the world) and many other treasures. Exeter was often visited by Elizabethan seamen such as Sir Francis Drake and Sir Walter Raleigh, who were both Devon men and knew the taverns of Exeter well - the Ship Inn is traditionally believed to have been one of Drake's favourite watering holes.

The city was a major centre for the Devon woollen industry, and exported finished cloth to France, Spain and the Netherlands. Its position by the River Exe gave it a reliable supply of water to power the industry; however, the trade declined as a result of the Industrial Revolution when steam-powered machines became the norm. Exeter was far from the coal supplies needed, and the cloth trade became focussed on the north of England. This meant that Exeter did not

become heavily industrialised or developed in the 19th century, and much of its historic city centre remained untouched until destroyed in the air-raids of the Second World War.

Exeter was heavily bombed during 'Baedeker raids' in 1942; these were raids deliberately aimed at some of the most historic British cities, chosen from the Baedeker guide books, and were an attempt by the Germans to lower British morale. As a result Exeter lost many of its historic buildings, although the cathedral and the ancient Guildhall still stand. However, enough remains to make Exeter a fascinating city to visit; this book can only give a glimpse of the colourful characters, events and stories that make up the city's history.

EXETER, HIGH STREET 1896 38012

DEVON DIALECT WORDS AND PHRASES

'Larrupin' – a good thumping, as in 'Stop, or I'll give 'e a gud larrupin'.

'My little maid' – my daughter.

'Lalager' – tongue.

'Aughts' – leftovers from meals.

'Dimpsy' – dusk, the early evening when it is getting dark.

'Tatties' – potatoes.

'ants' – as in 'all right, me ants?' – all right, my handsomes?

'Where be at?' – where are you?

'Frawzy' – a treat, as in 'Ev yerself a frawzy'.

'Like chapple a-pegs' – something sticking out like chapel hat pegs.

'Tiflin' – loose thread on clothing.

'zimzoiled' – ruined, spoiled.

'Dabbry' – droopy, wilted, floppy.

'Smitch' – a smoky atmosphere, like bonfire smoke or burnt toast in the kitchen.

'Crams' – nonsense or tantrums.

'Wallage' – a heap or pile of something.

'Chilliferous' – extremely cold.

'I'll lean on 'ee to do it praper' – I'll rely on you to do it right.

'What be on upon?' – a general greeting that covers everything from 'how are you'? to 'what have you been doing'? or 'what's going on here?'

'Demm' – the proper pronunciation of Devon, with a silent V!

HAUNTED EXETER

There have been several ghostly sightings at Exeter Cathedral. The cloisters are said to be haunted by phantom monks, and a mysterious figure of a nun has been spotted several times in the cloisters area, usually at around 7pm. She appears at a spot by the south wall of the nave, walks a short distance to the Church House, and vanishes. There is no story of tragedy or crime associated with this ghost, and as her head is bowed down she appears to be in prayer. The most recent sighting was by a group of French tourists to whom she appeared so clearly that they thought she was real, and made enquiries about which order she belonged to.

The Cowick Barton Inn in Cowick Lane stands on the former site of the monastery of St Thomas. The area around the inn is said to be haunted by the ghost of a monk, which has been seen in houses in Wellington Road, and also walking across the fields towards the river.

The Well House Tavern in Cathedral Close is apparently haunted by a friendly ghost known as 'Alice', who appears in a long white dress.

MISCELLANY

In his 'View of Devonshire' written in 1630, Thomas Westcote mentions the abundance of Devon orchards, particularly for the making of cider which he describes as being 'a drink both pleasant and healthy, much desired of seamen for long southern voyages as more fit to make beverage than beer, and much cheaper and easier to be had than wine.' Cider was a popular drink both at home and abroad; by 1820 11,265 hogsheads (each holding 63 gallons) of cider were shipped out from the ports of Exeter and Dartmouth.

APPLE TREE WASSAILING

In most cider-making counties a ceremony was held known as wassailing (from Anglo-Saxon 'Waes Hal', meaning 'good health'). This would be held in the winter, usually on Twelfth Night; jugs of cider were carried into the orchards, most of which would be drunk, and the rest would be poured around the roots of the apple trees. A lot of noise would be made with banging of pots and pans, to drive away evil spirits from the trees, and wake up the trees for the spring; sometimes shotguns would be fired through the branches. Special cakes would often be eaten, and pieces of cake or bread, soaked in cider, would be placed in the trees as a thanksgiving to the tree spirit, and to ensure a good crop in the following year.

Exeter's position on the River Exe made it a target for the Vikings (more correctly Danes), who attacked and captured the city in 876, before being driven out by King Alfred the Great.

COUNTESS WEAR, THE BRIDGE OVER THE EXE 1906 53981

In the winter of 1068 William the Conqueror besieged Exeter for eighteen days. It was the last town in England still to defy him after the Normans defeated the Anglo-Saxon King Harold at the Battle of Hastings two years earlier. Unbeknown to William, the town was sheltering King Harold's mother Gytha; she slipped out through the West Gate as the town surrendered and the Normans came in through the East Gate to claim their victory.

Countess Wear is a small village on the banks of the Exe, named after a 13th-century Countess of Devon who caused a weir to be constructed here which had serious implications for Exeter's economy. In the late 13th century the merchants of Exeter had a disastrous falling out with Lady Isabel, Countess of Devon. In retaliation she ordered a weir to be built across the Exe 3 miles south of the city, which obstructed access to Exeter's port. Although the Exeter people complained about this, the resulting legal dispute dragged on for almost 300 years. By the time that the city won the right to remove the weir the damage had been done: the river had silted up and trade had been badly affected. During the dispute Exeter was served by the port at Topsham.

EXETER CATHEDRAL, THE WEST FRONT 1887 19601

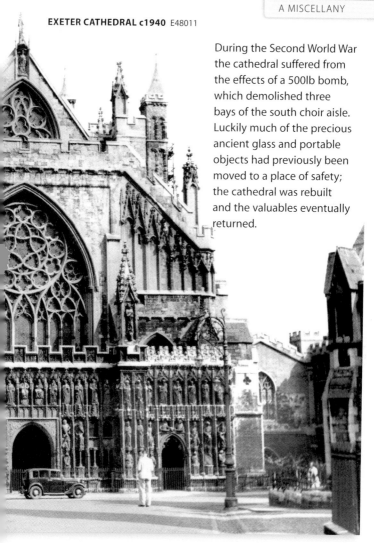

EXETER CATHEDRAL c1940 E48011

During the Second World War the cathedral suffered from the effects of a 500lb bomb, which demolished three bays of the south choir aisle. Luckily much of the precious ancient glass and portable objects had previously been moved to a place of safety; the cathedral was rebuilt and the valuables eventually returned.

EXETER, FORE STREET 1896 38008

Exeter's Lammas Fair dates back to Anglo-Saxon days. The name 'Lammas' comes from the Anglo-Saxon word 'Hlafmaesse', or 'Loaf Mass' and refers to the feast day of St Peter ad Vincula, when a loaf was given to the Church in a custom similar to present-day harvest festivals. The sheriff's coach which is on public display in the Civic Centre is used once a year by the mayor for the Lammas Fair, the position of sheriff having ceased in 1973/4.

After the 1685 rebellion of the Duke of Monmouth, the illegitimate son of Charles II, Judge Jeffreys held one of his Bloody Assizes in Exeter and sentenced 80 of the rebels to be hanged.

In 1497 the pretender Perkin Warbeck tried to enter Exeter with his army. He claimed to be Richard, Duke of York, the younger of the Princes in the Tower who had mysteriously disappeared during the reign of Richard III. He failed to get into Exeter at that time, but later succeeded in making an entry - in chains. Henry VII held him here before removing him to the Tower of London and a date with the executioner.

A detailed study of the carvings on Exeter Cathedral reveals English kings, priests and soldiers. Some of the kings are sitting cross-legged. Similar poses can be seen in the cathedrals of Lichfield and Lincoln. Angels, prophets and apostles are also depicted by those long-dead craftsmen.

EXETER CATHEDRAL, THE WEST FRONT 1924 76587A

In 1942 Exeter was the subject of one of Hitler's 'Baedeker' raids. These were air raids deliberately targeted at some of Britain's most historic cities, chosen from the Baedeker guidebooks. Their destruction was expected to weaken morale. On three successive nights in April, and again in May, bombs rained down on the city. 1,700 buildings, including some of the finest Regency houses in Exeter, were destroyed. A further 14,000 buildings were damaged, and civilian casualties were heavy.

The Bristol and Exeter Railway opened in 1844 and the continuation towards Torquay and Plymouth was opened in 1849. Exeter became a rail crossroads with branch lines to both north and south; with the arrival of the London and South Western Railway in 1860 this expansion continued as that company moved into northern Devon and Cornwall. In late years these lines would become known as 'the withered arm' of the Southern Railway.

Exeter cathedral is unique in that it has two twin Norman towers flanking the nave.

When repairs were being carried out on Exeter cathedral after the bombing raids of the Second World War, a collection of wax models was found in a cavity of a stone screen by the choir. The models were of humans and animals, mainly of limbs, but there was also a complete figure of a woman. It is thought that these were offerings given by pilgrims to the tomb of Bishop Edmund Lacy, left by people who had come to pray for the recovery of either themselves or of sick animals. The models are now kept in the Cathedral Library.

EXETER CATHEDRAL c1940 E48028

W.V. COLE & SONS PRINTERS

EXETER CATHEDRAL 1924 76579

Exeter's cathedral is the only cathedral in England that does not have a central tower, which allows the roof to run uninterrupted from end to end of the building, making it the longest stretch of Gothic vaulting in the world.

The Bishop's Throne in the cathedral is 60 feet high. It was carved from Devon oak in the early 14th century, and is one of the best examples of medieval carving in England. It does not contain any nails - everything is held together by wooden pins.

In Princehay, visitors can enter underground passages - these are not 'secret passages' but were dug in the 13th century to carry water around the town from local springs.

Rougemont Castle was one of the earliest Norman fortifications, established in 1068 by William the Conqueror. Most of the area is now ruins.

EXETER, ROUGEMONT CASTLE 1924 75980

After the cathedral, the Guildhall is probably the oldest building in Exeter. It was originally 13th-century, and was rebuilt 100 years

later. The portico overhanging the High Street was added during the reign of Elizabeth I.

EXETER, HIGH STREET AND THE GUILDHALL 1929 82291

Mol's Coffee House, seen from the outside, is essentially 17th-century, with the Dutch-style gable added around 1885. However, much of the interior is 16th-century, and it is known that Raleigh, Hawkins, Drake and other famous seafarers frequented this very building.

One fascinating story in the Exeter area is that of John 'Babbacombe' Lee, popularly known as 'the man they couldn't hang'. At a house called The Glen in the south Devon resort of Babbacombe, the elderly Miss Emma Keyse was found murdered in 1884. Her servant John Lee was accused of the crime and sentenced to death. Three times the hangman tried to execute Lee in Exeter Gaol; each time the trapdoor refused to open, and in the end John 'Babbacombe' Lee's sentence was commuted to life imprisonment. Some said that the failure was due to divine intervention, as Lee may have been innocent, 'set up' by a wealthy and influential Torquay gentleman who was the real murderer. A likelier explanation was that the wood of the 'drop' had swollen through exposure to damp weather. Lee was released from prison in 1907 and wrote his memoirs, becoming something of a celebrity.

The Met Office has recently moved to Exeter from Berkshire. This important weather forecasting organisation is expected to provide significant employment opportunities for the city.

Exeter acquired its first 'fire-engine' in 1626; this must have been seen as an improvement on the four dozen leather buckets and twelve ladders that were purchased by the city in 1559.

The Buller Statue is in memory of a local hero. Sir Redvers Henry Buller was born in Crediton in 1839 and served with the 60th Rifles. He was Commander-in-Chief in the 2nd Boer War (1899-1900) and raised the Siege of Ladysmith in 1900. He died in 1908, and the bronze statue was erected in 1905.

The side-saddle traveller Celia Fiennes came to Exeter in 1698 and recorded her impressions:

'Exeter is a town very well built. The streets are well pitched, spacious noble streets, and a vast trade is carried on … there is an incredible quantity of serges made and sold in the town. Their market day is Friday which supplies with all things like a fair almost. The market for meat, fowl, fish, garden things, and dairy produce takes up three whole streets, besides the large market house set on stone pillars which runs a great length, on which they lay their packs of serges. Just by it is another walk within pillars which is for the yarn. The whole town and country is employed for at least twenty miles around in spinning, weaving, dressing and scouring, fulling and drying of the serges. It turns the most money in a week of anything in England. One week with another, there is £10,000 paid in ready money, sometimes £15,000 ..'

In 1658 the journey from Exeter to London took 4 days; with improved roads following the General Turnpike Act of 1753 Exeter became a major centre for stagecoach travel. By 1785 the journey from Exeter to London could be done in 24 hours.

REDVERS BULLER
VC C.C.B. C.C.M.G
OF DOWNES

1859-1900
INDIA CHINA
CANADA ASHANTI
EGYPT SOUDAN
SOUTH AFRICA
HE SAVED NATAL

EXETER, THE PORT 1896 38034

A little-known fact is that Exeter was the first place in England to be served by an artificial canal with locks. This, constructed in 1564-66, pre-dated the canals in the north of England, where many people think the canal age started. It was built after the establishment of a weir in the 13th century at Countess Wear stopped the use of the river for trade. Final improvements on the Exeter Canal, completed in 1832, allowed larger vessels to reach the Port.

In 928 the city was renamed Exancaester by the Anglo-Saxon King Athelstan.

The Prayer Book Rebellion of 1549 was an uprising of Devon and Cornwall peasants protesting about the Act of Uniformity, which enforced the use of the Book of Common Prayer in English. The Roman Catholic peasants were demanding to be able to attend the old Latin mass. Their combined forces from Devon and Cornwall closed in on Exeter hoping for support from the city, but the mayor and corporation closed the city gates against them, and a siege began which lasted for five weeks. The citizens of Exeter were on the verge of starvation and surrender when the rebels moved away to fight against Lord Russell's forces at Fenny Bridge.

EXETER FROM THE CANAL 1929 82302

The Cathedral Library in the Bishop's Palace contains some important early manuscripts, including the Exon Domesday (1086) and the Exeter Book of Poetry (early 10th century).

EXETER, HIGH STREET 1896 38013

In 928 the Anglo-Saxon King Athelstan expelled the British (Celts) from the British quarter of Exeter so that it would become a Saxon town.

EXETER, THE CLOCK TOWER
1929 82298

Located at the junction of New North Road and Queen's Street, the Gothic creation of the Clock Tower was constructed as part of Queen Victoria's Diamond Jubilee celebrations in 1897 and was designed by T H Andrews.

The eminent landscape historian Dr W G Hoskins, author of 'The Making of the English Landscape', was born at 26-28 St David's Hill, Exeter. He was instrumental in forming the Exeter Group, which became the Exeter Civic Society.

On the side of Topshop in Exeter's High Street is a mural with three figures on it - one of these is Princess Henrietta Anne, who was born in Exeter whilst her mother, Charles I's wife, Queen Henrietta Maria, was sheltering in the city during the Civil War. In the Guildhall is a full-length portrait of the Princess, given to the city in 1671 by her brother King Charles II.

Exeter grew rich on the Devon woollen cloth industry. The cloth was woven throughout the county, but was dyed and finished in Exeter before being exported to France, Spain and the Netherlands. The reliable water source provided by the River Exe was a major factor in the success of this industry.

The River Exe is Devon's main river. It rises in north Devon, on Exmoor, and flows south for almost 50 miles before reaching the sea at Exmouth. In 1924 a salmon weighing 64lb was caught in the River Exe by fisherman Richard Voysey.

Stepcote Hill links Exeter city with the Exe valley. At the bottom is 'The House that Moved'; this historic local building was in the path of a road scheme, and was carefully excavated and rolled some 400 yards to its new position. St Mary Steps Church, on Stepcote Hill, has a clock in its wall in which the hours are struck by three figures, known locally as Matthew the Miller and his two sons.

The famous naval mutiny at the Nore (1797) was led by the seaman Richard Parker, who was born in Exeter in about 1767. The sailors' 'Floating Republic', which included thirteen ships of the line, blockaded the River Thames and refused to put to sea unless certain grievances were put right. The Naval authorities crushed the mutiny and on 30 June 1797 Parker was hanged at the yard-arm.

Daniel Defoe came to Exeter in 1714 and wrote: 'Tis full of gentry and good company, and yet full of trade and manufacture also. The serge market held here every week is very well worth a stranger seeing, and next to the Brigg market at Leeds in Yorkshire, is the greatest in England. The people assured me that at this market is generally sold from 60 to 70 to 80, and sometimes a hundred thousand pounds'.

Jane Austen's happy memories of a holiday in south Devon caused her to set 'Sense and Sensibility' in the area. Her first novel, written in 1811, saw the two Dashwood sisters come to live in the village of Upton Pyne, about four miles from Exeter. In the book, the marriage of Elinor Dashwood and Edward Ferrers was set in the village church.

Did You Know?
EXETER
A MISCELLANY

EXETER FROM THE CANAL 1896 38033

Chris Martin, of the award winning group Coldplay, was born in Exeter in 1977.

The first landing at Exeter airport took place on 10 May 1937 when films of the coronation of HM King George VI were flown in to be shown in the cinemas of Exeter. Exeter airport was officially opened on 31 May 1937. The first airliner to use the airport was greeted by the Mayor of Exeter, Alfred Anstey. The Mayor and civic leaders were then given a flight over the city.

There are seventeen towns called Exeter in the USA.

During the Second World War 307 Squadron of the Polish Air Force was stationed at Exeter and operated night fighters. The squadron was known locally as 'Defenders of Exeter'.

Five Royal Navy warships have carried the name HMS 'Exeter'. Earlier ships were involved in the Battle of the River Plate and the sinking of the German battleship 'Graf Spee' in 1939. The current HMS 'Exeter' is a type 42 destroyer; it was launched in 1979, and saw service in the Falklands War in 1982. Like the city, the motto of HMS 'Exeter' is 'semper fidelis'.

EXETER, THE ROYAL CLARENCE HOTEL AND DELLAR'S CAFÉ 1907 58031

Although much of the west of England was for King Charles I during the Civil War, Exeter, like many ports, was on the side of Parliament. However the city was captured by Royalists on

EXETER, ST MARY STEPS CHURCH 1912 64577

4 September 1643, and was made the Royalist headquarters in the west. Exeter remained under Royalist control until, after a siege in1645/6, it was successfully taken back by Parliamentarian forces.

TOPSHAM, DUTCH HOUSES, THE STRAND c1965 T59007

There is a strong Dutch influence in much of the housing in Topsham, especially on the Strand. Dutch trading ships, which docked to load Exeter cloth, brought in bricks as ballast, and these were used by the local merchants with Dutch architecture in mind.

On the tomb of John Tully, a mayor of Exeter, in Exeter Cathedral:

Here lies the body of Captain Tully,

Aged a hundred and nine years fully;

And threescore years before, as mayor,

The sword of this city he did bear.

Nine of his wives do by him lie,

So shall the tenth when she doth die!

EXETER, THE RIVER EXE AND THE BRIDGE 1929 82301

George Gissing, the Victorian novelist and journalist, summed up the atmosphere of Topsham in 'The Private Papers of Henry Ryecroft': '...a long ramble hour after hour entirely enjoyable. It ended at Topsham, where I sat on the little churchyard terrace,

TOPSHAM, THE QUAY 1906 53990

and watched the evening tide come up the broad estuary. I have a great liking for Topsham, and that churchyard overlooking what is not quite sea, yet more than river, is one of the most restful spots I know.'

EXETER, OLD HOUSES 1924 76592

SPORTING EXETER

On 14 June 2002 the singer Michael Jackson visited St James' Park to support Exeter City FC at the invitation of his friend Uri Geller, co-chairman of the club. Michael offered to help out at a fund-raising day for the club and local charities, and arrived in the ground in a vintage car to address over 10,000 fans. He said in his speech that he knew nothing about football, but was backing England in the World Cup.

The nickname of Exeter City Football Club, one of the most unusual and distinctive in football, is 'the Grecians'. The name derives from the people of the parish of St Sidwell, known for centuries as 'Greeks' - although the reason for this name has several interpretations. St Sidwellian Old Boys were co-founders of Exeter City in 1904.

The football player Alan Ball, who was in the England World Cup winning team in 1966, managed the Grecians in the 1992-94 seasons. When Exeter were drawn against Aston Villa in the FA Cup he famously remarked: 'I've seen Desert Orchid fall, I've seen Bestie refuse a drink, I've seen Emlyn Hughes buy one, so you never know'.

One of Exeter's greatest football heroes is Cliff Bastin, who was born in Heavitree in 1912. He first played for Exeter City in 1928, at the age of 16. He joined Arsenal in 1929 and played for the Gunners until 1947, scoring 150 League goals. He played for England 21 times, finishing his international career in 1938. He held the record as Arsenal's highest goal scorer until beaten by Ian Wright in the 1990s. After retirement Cliff Bastin ran the Horse and Groom at Heavitree, and died in 1991.

Exeter racecourse is the highest (850 ft) and second longest (2 miles) in the country. There has been racing here since the reign of Charles II. Notable horses to have begun their careers here include Desert Orchid and Best Mate, both of which went on to become winners of the Cheltenham Gold Cup.

Exeter City FC made a historic tour to South America in 1914; whilst there they played matches in Argentina and Brazil. They became the first club side to play the Brazilian national team.

QUIZ QUESTIONS

Answers on page 49.

1. What is believed to lie underneath the present High Street?

2. What was special about Exeter's Customs House?

3. The area around the Customs House has often been used as a location for films and television programmes, including which very popular TV shipping drama of the 1970s?

4. Which piece of Antarctic memorabilia can be found in Exeter Cathedral?

5. Can you name the four towns that are twinned with Exeter?

6. What is Exeter's motto, and who suggested it?

7. Which drinking hole in Exeter is believed to have been a favourite of Sir Francis Drake?

8. What has Exeter contributed to the Crown Jewels?

9. The author Thomas Hardy knew Exeter well, and his close friend Tryphena Sparks is buried in Topsham churchyard. Hardy referred to Exeter, under a different name, in four of his novels. What did he call it, and which novels are they?

10. Who described the Exeter area as 'the most beautiful in this most beautiful of English counties'?

43

RECIPE

EXETER PUDDING

Mrs Beeton included a recipe for Exeter Pudding in her Book of Household Management.

Ingredients:

10oz (275g) of bread crumbs

4oz (115g) of sago

7oz (200g) of finely-chopped suet

6oz (175g) of moist sugar

The rind of half a lemon

A quarter pint of rum (150ml)

7 eggs

4 tablespoonfuls of cream

4 small sponge cakes

2oz (50g) of ratafia biscuits

Half a pound of jam (8oz, or a small-size jar)

Put the bread crumbs into a basin with the sago, suet, sugar, minced lemon-peel, rum and 4 eggs; stir these ingredients well together, then add 3 more eggs and the cream, and let the mixture be well beaten. Then butter a mould, strew in a few bread crumbs, and cover the bottom with a layer of ratafias; then put in a layer of the mixture, then a layer of sliced sponge cake spread thickly with any kind of jam; then add some ratafias, then some of the mixture and sponge cake, and so on until the mould is full, taking care that a layer of the mixture is on the top of the pudding. Bake in a good oven from three-quarter to 1 hour, and serve with the following sauce:

Put 3 tablespoonfuls of black-currant jelly into a stewpan, add 2 glasses of sherry, and, when warm, turn the pudding out of the mould, pour the sauce over it, and serve hot.

TOPSHAM, THE CHURCH 1906 53994

RECIPE

CIDER CAKE

Ingredients:

250g/8oz mixed sultanas, raisins and currants

4 tablespoons sweet cider

175g/6oz butter or margarine

175g/6oz soft brown sugar

3 eggs

250g/8oz self-raising flour

1 teaspoon mixed spice (optional)

Soak the mixed fruits in the cider overnight. Cream the butter
or margarine and add the sugar. Cream until fluffy. Lightly
beat the eggs and gradually beat them into the mixture. Mix
in the fruit and cider. Sift the flour and spice together, fold
in half of the flour, and mix well. Mix in the rest of the flour.
Grease a 20cm/8 inch round or 18cm/7 inch square tin and
line the bottom with greased, greaseproof paper. Bake in a
moderate oven, gas mark 4, 350 degrees F, 180 degrees C, for
1 hour and 10 minutes.

EXETER, HIGH STREET AND POST OFFICE 1896 38011

QUIZ ANSWERS

1. A Roman road.

2. It was the first brick house to be built in the city.

3. 'The Onedin Line'.

4. Captain Robert Falcon Scott's sledge flag from his 1900 Antarctic expedition hangs in the nave of Exeter Cathedral.

5. Rennes (France), Bad Homburg (Germany), Yaroslavl (Russia) and Terracina (Italy).

6. Exeter's motto 'semper fidelis' (ever faithful) was suggested by Queen Elizabeth I, after the citizens raised a sum of money towards defeating the Armada.

7. The Ship Inn, in Martin's Lane, just off Cathedral Green, is traditionally believed to have been one of Sir Francis Drake's favourite taverns.

8. Amongst the Crown Jewels is a magnificent silver gilt table salt, which the citizens of Exeter gave to Charles II after the restoration of the monarchy in 1660.

9. Thomas Hardy called Exeter 'Exonbury', and there are references to it in 'The Trumpet Major', 'Jude the Obscure', 'A Pair of Blue Eyes' and 'The Woodlanders'.

10. Charles Dickens. His parents lived at Mile End Cottage in Aphington for four years. Dickens wrote the opening chapters of Nicholas Nickleby there.

TOPSHAM, THE STRAND 1906 53993

FRANCIS FRITH

PIONEER VICTORIAN PHOTOGRAPHER

Francis Frith, founder of the world-famous photographic archive, was a complex and multi-talented man. A devout Quaker and a highly successful Victorian businessman, he was philosophical by nature and pioneering in outlook. By 1855 he had already established a wholesale grocery business in Liverpool, and sold it for the astonishing sum of £200,000, which is the equivalent today of over £15,000,000. Now in his thirties, and captivated by the new science of photography, Frith set out on a series of pioneering journeys up the Nile and to the Near East.

INTRIGUE AND EXPLORATION

He was the first photographer to venture beyond the sixth cataract of the Nile. Africa was still the mysterious 'Dark Continent', and Stanley and Livingstone's historic meeting was a decade into the future. The conditions for picture taking confound belief. He laboured for hours in his wicker dark-room in the sweltering heat of the desert, while the volatile chemicals fizzed dangerously in their trays. Back in London he exhibited his photographs and was 'rapturously cheered' by members of the Royal Society. His reputation as a photographer was made overnight.

VENTURE OF A LIFE-TIME

By the 1870s the railways had threaded their way across the country, and Bank Holidays and half-day Saturdays had been made obligatory by Act of Parliament. All of a sudden the working man and his family were able to enjoy days out, take holidays, and see a little more of the world.

With typical business acumen, Francis Frith foresaw that these new tourists would enjoy having souvenirs to commemorate their days out. For the next thirty years he travelled the country by train and by pony and trap, producing fine photographs of seaside resorts and beauty spots that were keenly bought by millions of Victorians. These prints were painstakingly pasted into family albums and pored over during the dark nights of winter, rekindling precious memories of summer excursions. Frith's studio was soon supplying retail shops all over the country, and by 1890 F Frith & Co had become the greatest specialist photographic publishing company in the world, with over 2,000 sales outlets, and pioneered the picture postcard.

FRANCIS FRITH'S LEGACY

Francis Frith had died in 1898 at his villa in Cannes, his great project still growing. By 1970 the archive he created contained over a third of a million pictures showing 7,000 British towns and villages.

Frith's legacy to us today is of immense significance and value, for the magnificent archive of evocative photographs he created provides a unique record of change in the cities, towns and villages throughout Britain over a century and more. Frith and his fellow studio photographers revisited locations many times down the years to update their views, compiling for us an enthralling and colourful pageant of British life and character.

We are fortunate that Frith was dedicated to recording the minutiae of everyday life. For it is this sheer wealth of visual data, the painstaking chronicle of changes in dress, transport, street layouts, buildings, housing and landscape that captivates us so much today, offering us a powerful link with the past and with the lives of our ancestors.

Computers have now made it possible for Frith's many thousands of images to be accessed almost instantly. The archive offers every one of us an opportunity to examine the places where we and our families have lived and worked down the years. Its images, depicting our shared past, are now bringing pleasure and enlightenment to millions around the world a century and more after his death.

For further information visit: www.francisfrith.com

INTERIOR DECORATION

Frith's photographs can be seen framed and as giant wall murals in thousands of pubs, restaurants, hotels, banks, retail stores and other public buildings throughout Britain. These provide interesting and attractive décor, generating strong local interest and acting as a powerful reminder of gentler days in our increasingly busy and frenetic world.

FRITH PRODUCTS

All Frith photographs are available as prints and posters in a variety of different sizes and styles. In the UK we also offer a range of other gift and stationery products illustrated with Frith photographs, although many of these are not available for delivery outside the UK – see our web site for more information on the products available for delivery in your country.

THE INTERNET

Over 100,000 photographs of Britain can be viewed and purchased on the Frith web site. The web site also includes memories and reminiscences contributed by our customers, who have personal knowledge of localities and of the people and properties depicted in Frith photographs. If you wish to learn more about a specific town or village you may find these reminiscences fascinating to browse. Why not add your own comments if you think they would be of interest to others? See **www.francisfrith.com**

PLEASE HELP US BRING FRITH'S PHOTOGRAPHS TO LIFE

Our authors do their best to recount the history of the places they write about. They give insights into how particular towns and villages developed, they describe the architecture of streets and buildings, and they discuss the lives of famous people who lived there. But however knowledgeable our authors are, the story they tell is necessarily incomplete.

Frith's photographs are so much more than plain historical documents. They are living proofs of the flow of human life down the generations. They show real people at real moments in history; and each of those people is the son or daughter of someone, the brother or sister, aunt or uncle, grandfather or grandmother of someone else. All of them lived, worked and played in the streets depicted in Frith's photographs.

We would be grateful if you would give us your insights into the places shown in our photographs: the streets and buildings, the shops, businesses and industries. Post your memories of life in those streets on the Frith website: what it was like growing up there, who ran the local shop and what shopping was like years ago; if your workplace is shown tell us about your working day and what the building is used for now. Read other visitors' memories and reconnect with your shared local history and heritage. With your help more and more Frith photographs can be brought to life, and vital memories preserved for posterity, and for the benefit of historians in the future.

Wherever possible, we will try to include some of your comments in future editions of our books. Moreover, if you spot errors in dates, titles or other facts, please let us know, because our archive records are not always completely accurate—they rely on 140 years of human endeavour and hand-compiled records. You can email us using the contact form on the website.

Thank you!

For further information, trade, or author enquiries
please contact us at the address below:

**The Francis Frith Collection, Frith's Barn, Teffont,
Salisbury, Wiltshire, England SP3 5QP.**

Tel: +44 (0)1722 716 376 Fax: +44 (0)1722 716 881
e-mail: sales@francisfrith.co.uk **www.francisfrith.com**